CAPE POETRY PAPERBACKS

ADRIAN HENRI
THE BEST OF HENRI

By the Same Author

TONIGHT AT NOON
CITY
THE MERSEY SOUND
(with Roger McGough and Brian Patten)
I WANT (with Nell Dunn)
AUTOBIOGRAPHY
ENVIRONMENTS AND HAPPENINGS

Adrian Henri

THE BEST OF HENRI

SELECTED POEMS 1960–70

JONATHAN CAPE
THIRTY BEDFORD SQUARE LONDON

for Joyce Henri
and
Susan Sterne

First published 1975
This paperback edition first published 1975
© 1967, 1968, 1969, 1970, 1971, 1975 by Adrian Henri

Jonathan Cape Ltd,
30 Bedford Square, London WCI

ISBN 0 224 01148 0

A number of the poems in this book were
first published in the following volumes: *The
Mersey Sound* (Penguin Modern Poets, 1967);
Tonight at Noon (Rapp & Whiting, 1968);
City (Rapp & Whiting, 1969). The author and
publisher are grateful for permission to reprint
them here.

Printed in Great Britain by
Ebenezer Baylis & Son Ltd.,
The Trinity Press, Worcester and London

Contents

ME
if you weren't you, who would you like to be?

Paul McCartney Gustav Mahler
Alfred Jarry John Coltrane
Charlie Mingus Claude Debussy
Wordsworth Monet Bach and Blake

Charlie Parker Pierre Bonnard
Leonardo Bessie Smith
Fidel Castro Jackson Pollock
Gaudi Milton Munch and Berg

Belà Bartók Henri Rousseau
Rauschenberg and Jasper Johns
Lukas Cranach Shostakovich
Kropotkin Ringo George and John

William Burroughs Francis Bacon
Dylan Thomas Luther King
H. P. Lovecraft T. S. Eliot
D. H. Lawrence Roland Kirk

Salvatore Giuliano
Andy Warhol Paul Cézanne
Kafka Camus Ensor Rothko
Jacques Prévert and Manfred Mann

Marx Dostoievsky
Bakunin Ray Bradbury
Miles Davis Trotsky
Stravinsky and Poe

Danilo Dolci Napoleon Solo
St John of the Cross and
The Marquis de Sade

Charles Rennie Mackintosh
Rimbaud Claes Oldenburg
Adrian Mitchell and Marcel Duchamp

James Joyce and Hemingway
Hitchcock and Buñuel
Donald McKinlay Thelonius Monk

Alfred, Lord Tennyson
Matthias Grünewald
Philip Jones Griffiths and Roger McGough

Guillaume Apollinaire
Cannonball Adderley
René Magritte
Hieronymus Bosch

Stéphane Mallarmé and Alfred de Vigny
Ernst Mayakovsky and Nicolas de Staël
Hindemith Mick Jagger Dürer and Schwitters
Garcia Lorca
            and
                last of all
                    me.

SIX LANDSCAPES FOR SUSAN

1

You
in the country
looking at horses
picking deadly nightshade
observing lesser celandines

2

Pools by factories applegreen
and bright with rainbows

3

Slow doubledecker bus
moving between
red dead mountain bracken
and thin trees veiling the valley
dotted with farms

4

Walking
round a village corner
turning into a doorway
in a large hoarding
into darkness stone stairs smelling of apples
out
into the early morning the
air dazzling with the cries of seagulls
mountain slopes
reared up at the end of the tiny street

5

Bright green ferns through raingrey sky
round railway tunnels in Yorkshire
pale pink roses picked for you
after pie and chips in late night Oldham cafés

6

Palegreen fields powdered with yellow flowers
two cutout men in white with buckets
carrying a sign across a sunlit field
swollen rivers and shining watermeadows
one lapwing
swans
cows wading up to their ankles
poppies in clumps of grass
on purple gravel by the railway line

THE ENTRY OF CHRIST INTO LIVERPOOL

City morning. dandelionseeds   blowing from wasteground.
smell of overgrown privethedges. children's voices
in the distance. sounds from the river.
round the corner into Myrtle St. Saturdaymorning shoppers
headscarves. shoppingbaskets. dogs.

then
   down the hill

             THE SOUND OF TRUMPETS
          cheering and shouting in the distance
                  children running
                    icecream vans
            flags breaking out over buildings
            black and red green and yellow
               Union Jacks Red Ensigns
          LONG LIVE SOCIALISM
             stretched against the blue sky
                over St George's hall

Now the procession

          THE MARCHING DRUMS
hideous masked Breughel faces of old ladies in the crowd
   yellow masks of girls in curlers and headscarves
                smelling of factories
               Masks Masks Masks
        red masks purple masks pink masks

         crushing surging carrying me along

down the hill past the Philharmonic The Labour Exchange
excited feet crushing the geraniums in St Luke's Gardens
placards banners posters
Keep Britain White
End the War in Vietnam
God Bless Our Pope
Billboards hoardings drawings on pavements
words painted on the road
STOP GO HALT
the sounds of pipes and drums down the street
little girls in yellow and orange dresses paper flowers
embroidered banners
Loyal Sons of King William Lodge, Bootle
Masks more Masks crowding in off buses
standing on walls climbing fences

familiar faces among the crowd
faces of my friends the shades of Pierre Bonnard and
Guillaume Apollinaire
Jarry cycling carefully through the crowd. A black cat
picking her way underfoot
posters
signs
gleaming salads
COLMANS MUSTARD
J. Ensor, Fabriqueur de Masques
HAIL JESUS, KING OF THE JEWS
straining forward to catch a glimpse through the crowd
red hair white robe grey donkey
familiar face
trafficlights zebracrossings
GUIN
GUINN
GUINNESS IS

white bird dying unnoticed in a corner
splattered feathers
blood running merged with the neonsigns
in a puddle
GUINNESS IS GOOD
GUINNESS IS GOOD FOR
Masks Masks Masks Masks Masks
GUINNESS IS GOOD FOR YOU

brassbands cheering loudspeakers blaring
clatter of police horses
ALL POWER TO THE CONSTITUENT
ASSEMBLY
masks cheering glittering teeth
daffodils trodden underfoot

BUTCHERS OF JERUSALEM
banners cheering drunks stumbling and singing
masks
masks
masks

evening
thin sickle moon
pale blue sky
flecked with bright orange clouds
streamers newspapers discarded paper hats
blown slowly back up the hill by the evening wind
dustmen with big brooms sweeping the gutters
last of the crowds waiting at bus-stops
giggling schoolgirls quiet businessmen
me
walking home
empty chip-papers drifting round my feet.

SEE THE CONKERING HEROINE COMES

Thinking about you
Walking the woods in Autumn
jumping for branches picking glossy horse-chestnuts
                           from the ground
caught purple-handed coming back from blackberrying
Walking handinhand in the summer park
flowers dropping on you as we walk through the palm-
                              house.

magenta to pink to faded rose
pink hearts floating on tiny waterfalls
the woods echoing to the song of the Mersey Bowmen
leaves you said were the colour of the green sweets
                       in Mackintosh's Weekend
cheeks warm and smooth like peaches not apples
hair caught golden in the sunlight
your child's eyes wondering at the colour of
                          rhododendrons
and the whiteness of swans.

Coming back in Autumn
the air loud with the colours of Saturdayafternoon
                             football
the alleyway of trees they planted for us in summer
still there
young appletrees going to sleep in their applepie beds
tropical plants in the palmhouse you said
looked like lions sticking their tongues out
one faded pink flower left
leaves falling very slowly in the tropical afternoon inside
you suddenly seeing a family of mice
living high up in the painted wroughtiron girders.

Walking back
the lakes cold the rhododendrons shivering slightly in
                                        the dusk
peacocks closing up their tails 'til next summer
your hand in mine
the first frost of winter touching your cheeks.

WINTERPOEM
(for Elizabeth)

See the conquering hero winter comes
Frost on the palmhouse windows mist covering the
                                        flowerbeds
Swans somehow not frozen into their lakes
Taking our walk instead in the city
Out of the warm
Neat   O'Cedar floor you just polished

Snow up steps corrugated-iron door black wall
Cathedral disappeared into the mist
Only the railings hard fringed with white like the laurel-
                                        leaves
Tiny drops of water frozen before falling
Snow stained pink with ash round doorstep and dustbins
Railings
Pagoda in the square Japanese with willow trees for us
Violet cellophane sweet paper singing against pavement
                                        snow

Cold hands through woolly gloves

Writing this in summer wondering
Where are the snows of yesterday?

I SUPPOSE YOU THINK IT'S FUNNY

I suppose you think it's funny
when your smile opens me like a tin of Kit-E-Kat
I suppose you think it's funny
when perfumed dancers with sequinned tights
fill my Arabian Nights with Turkish Delights
I suppose you think it's funny
when your nightdress falls open revealing last year's
                              election posters
I suppose you think it's funny
to post the cat and put out my poems instead
I suppose you think it's funny
to hang a photograph of Eichmann over your bed
signed *"Affectionately yours, Adolf"*
I suppose you think it's funny
when the bath breaks out in limegreen spots before my
                              astonished gaze
I suppose you think it's funny
to give away the time we've spent to a door-to-door
                              Ancient of days
I suppose you think it's funny
to publish my secret identity in the *Liverpool Echo*
I suppose you think it's funny
to fill my Y-fronts with Red Kryptonite
I suppose you think it's funny
to comb your hair like a lion
and push my breakfast through the bars
I suppose you think it's funny
to fill the next door garden with schoolgirls playing guitars
I suppose you think it's funny
when I cover you with flowers
I suppose you think it's funny
when you take an April shower
I suppose you think it's funny

when you've taken all my money
and the bailiff's in the parlour
eating bread and honey
and you meet me in a thunderstorm
and tell me that it's sunny
I suppose *you* think it's funny.

LOVE POEM

East Lancs Road Poems   Snow scattering on the windscreen/blowing
from the drystone moors/I think of you.

My central nervous system has gone: my
ganglia aren't even on the AA map. My
     heart is
single-line traffic, one way only.

London Poems   On the tube after seeing Rauschenberg
the tube a huge construction where he had
     cunningly
          got people reflected in the windows and
          posters moving past

You and Père Ubu holding hands in Piccadilly
Walking off into the COCA COLA sunset

'Heather Holden, 16, Haslingden Grammar School "Haslingden Moors with Snow"   Beautiful/Hair falling over eyes/hands cold
          holding sketchbook/
crowded noisy schoolroom/postercolours/tiny
          blue uniform
frozen at the corner of a field/waiting to meet
          her first lover after school

Hate Poem   'To know know know you
Is to love love love you'
And I don't.

Love Poem   ANY RECORD IN THE TOP 20 ANYTIME
                    IS OUR TUNE

18

*Assemblage
of Objects
and
Mementoes*

An empty Colgate tube
An almond with ALMOND written on it
breakfastpink gingham shirt & red waistcoat
like

tomatoes
a bar of rock lettered all through with your
name

and a plastic flower
a pair of your old navyblue schooldrawers
an empty Drambuie bottle & an empty packet
of

export cigarettes
a signed copy of this poem
a chocolate Easter Egg

*'Bluetit
Patrol 2nd
15th
Rossendale
Girl Guides'
Summer
Camp
Arnside 1960'*

A photograph:
Little smiling girl in bra and knickers sitting
in a summer field
A red bra with I LOVE YOU written inside one
of

the cups
A painting of a shocking pink heart with your
name

scratched on it
Some rusting scissors and a decaying fan from
a dead

King's treasurehouse.

*Manchester
Poem*

Our love is watched over by all my masters;
Picabia watches from his cacodynamic eye
Max Ernst looks on as impersonally as when
he

watched
the Virgin Mary spanking the infant Jesus
Guillaume Apollinaire in Piccadilly Bus
Station

watches the unlikely couple walking the cold
streets

19

Monk takes his hands off the keyboard and
                                              smiles
           approvingly
The Beatles sing lullabys for our never-to-
                                          happen
           children
Quietly in the shadows by Central Station

William Burroughs sits dunking Pound Cake
                                        in coffee
           waiting for the last connection
and sees us through the window
Bartok has orchestrated the noise of the tulips
                                                  in
           Piccadilly Gardens for us
Marcel Duchamp has added your photograph
                                               to
           the Green Box
Dylan Thomas staggers into the Cromwell for
                                              one
           last one
and waves across to us
Kurt Schwitters smiles as he picks up the two
                                             pink
           bus tickets
we have just thrown away
Parker blows another chorus of Loverman for
                                              us
Ensor smiles behind his mask
Jarry cycles slowly behind us down Spring
                                         Gardens

Rauschenberg and Jasper Johns
Bless the bed we lie upon

Lakeland
Poem   Daffodils grow in the shadows of your hair
Waterfalls in the hollows of your throat
Your body a bright lake seen between houses
        catching the morning sun
Pale lilies-of-the-valley in the darkness of your
        thighs

Boots   I've had 3 new prs. of boots since I met you
And I keep thinking perhaps I should get a
    new relationship as well
But I don't need to:
Perhaps it's the kind that doesn't wear out.

Lawn   I think of you
Even when walking with beautiful girls
On the lawn of rich men's houses at night
Where the sky is mowed every morning
And the stars are switched on when the guests
        arrive

Commercial
    Kisses
        better for headaches than Aspirin alone.

Spring Poem
for
Heather   'I'm going to London tomorrow' you said
'And it will be Spring'
But that was last night
And today it's snowing.

Liverpool   Wind blowing inland from the Pierhead
Poem   I was glad to be seen with you in Liverpool
Dead ferryboats in the shadows between your
        hair
    and cheek.

THE NEW, FAST, AUTOMATIC DAFFODILS
(New variation on Wordsworth's 'Daffodils')

I wandered lonely as
THE NEW, FAST DAFFODIL
   FULLY AUTOMATIC
that floats on high o'er vales and hills
The Daffodil is generously dimensioned to accommodate
                                      four adult passengers
10,000 saw I at a glance
Nodding their new anatomically shaped heads in sprightly
                                        dance
Beside the lake beneath the trees
   in three bright modern colours
red, blue and pigskin
The Daffodil de luxe is equipped with a host of useful
                                      accessories
including windscreen wiper and washer with joint control
A Daffodil doubles the enjoyment of touring at home or abroad

in vacant or in pensive mood
SPECIFICATION:
    Overall width   1·44m (57″)
    Overall height   1·38m (54·3″)
    Max. speed   105 km/hr (65m.p.h.)
     (also cruising speed)
DAFFODIL
   RELIABLE − ECONOMICAL
DAFFODIL
   THE BLISS OF SOLITUDE
DAFFODIL
  The Variomatic Inward Eye
Travelling by Daffodil you can relax and enjoy every mile
                                      of the journey.

(Cut-up of Wordsworth's poem plus Dutch motor-car leaflet)

UNIVERSES
(for Edward Lucie-Smith)

2 Poems for H. P. Lovecraft

1

Miskatonic river
Flowing through a landscape that is always evening
Accusing eyes
in the empty streets of Innsmouth
Strange movements out on the reef
Tumuli on hilltops
Trembling in the thunder
Behind the gambrel roofs of Arkham.

2

'Ph'nglui mgw'nafh Cthulhu R'lyeh wgah'nagl fhtagn'

'In his house at R'lyeh
Great Cthulhu sleeps'

amid
alien geometries
perspectives
walls shifting as you watch them
slumbering
in the Cyclopean dripping gloom
waiting to wake like Leviathan
when his children shall call him.

Four Lovepoems for Ray Bradbury

1

sitting
holding your eight hands
on the bank of the dry red canal

2   (for Mike Evans)

you toss your long hair
and look at me with witcheyes

you kiss me
and disappear

my heart bursting
like an April balloon.

3

'And I'll always remember
the first time we went out together'
Your eyes misty behind the glass
Earthlight shining in your hair

4

the day before the Carnival leaves town.

a shy dwarf
waiting by the boardwalk
for the beautiful dancer
who never comes

Poem for Gully Foyle

> 'Gully Foyle is my name
> Terra is my nation
> Deep space is my dwelling place
> And Death's my destination'

> Alfred Bester, *Tiger! Tiger!*

Gouffre Martel. Darkness.
Under the rock and earth a voice
Lying your tigerface blazing in the dark
Listening to her
Your mind still trapped in the broken spaceship

Flaming man appearing like your vengeance
On the beach, in the 3-ring cosmic circus
Your scarred body your tattooed face
Leaping between Aldebaran and Ceres
Eternity at your feet. The stars your destination.

HOLCOMBE POEM/
POEM FOR A GIRL I DIDN'T MEET

walking on the moors thinking about how I didn't meet
    you yesterday
heather underfoot and mist over Pendle
the moor changing like an animal/brown to green grey to
    purple with the weather
sky blue at the edges
                        like a letter that came too late.

. . . Undine rising from the waters her golden hair
dripping in the moonlight . . . dead bird on a fence blood
dripping from its neck . . . Isis searching the rushes
for her murdered lover . . . small girl with a fishingrod
in a rushing valley full of ferns . . . the last supper
followed by the Four Just Desserts . . . watching the
white mocking figure at the edge of the Dark Forest
. . . beating naked blondhaired girls with
longstemmed purple flowers . . . Osiris judging
the dead mist rising up the valley seaweed tangled
in her moonlight hair . . .

trains
    moving through valleys
chimneys
    springing from hillsides
streams
    tumbling through boulders
clouds
    tilting from the horizon
and
    me
      on the moors
thinking about the girl I never met.

POEMS FOR WALES

1 icegreen
    mountain streams
      fresher
        than toothpaste
          cleaner tasting
            than menthol cigarettes

2 Gelert's grave
  used to make me cry like a baby
  now
  they're killing Vietnamese
  instead

3 standing
  looking at the landscape
  then
  signing it at the bottom
  in the snow on a petrol-station wall

4 thinking about you
      here
        in the country
          trying to spray the moon silver
          and
            only hitting the clouds

5 two lots of footprints
    through the snow
      to my room
    both of them
      mine

Short Poems

LOVE POEM/COLOUR SUPPLEMENT

It was our first great war
And after the first successful sortie
Into the nomansgland
between her thighs
We waited anxiously every month
for poppysellers to appear in her streets.

DRINKING SONG

He became more and more drunk
As the afternoon wore off.

SONG FOR A BEAUTIFUL GIRL PETROL-PUMP ATTENDANT ON THE MOTORWAY

I wanted your soft verges
But you gave me the hard shoulder.

POEM FOR ROGER McGOUGH

A nun in a Supermarket
Standing in the queue
Wondering what it's like
To buy groceries for two.

DAWN CHORUS

If I were a blackbird
I'd whistle and sing
And stay in bed until eleven in the morning.

SATURDAY (for Philip Jones Griffiths).

I spent Saturday
feeling randy
drinking brandy reading *Candy*
to Brahms's Violin Concerto.

FAIRGROUND POEM

My mind is a fairground
Noise-Gaiety-Bright
colours, at the back
THE VAMPIRES CAVE
huge bats with horrible
wings like old umbrellas
(but the vampires are really fruitbats
and live on old mouldy peaches the punters won't buy)
And the FUN HOUSE with the beautiful dark-eyed
                                        Madonna
who smiles at me but is married to someone else
And pimply girls in cowboy hats
THE CISCO KID emerge and lascivious compressed air blows
                                        up their skirts
(sometimes they cross this part three or four times)
Beautiful little girls of 12 or 13 in enormous sunglasses
With beautiful tight little arses
(like two plums in a wet paper bag)
and firm little tits like toffee apples 6d.
she smiles at me sexily (holding her mother's
arm) her mouth bursting with little even teeth.
knowing I want to have her and can't
(*'Don't be a burke, you'd get your collar felt'*)
And always in my mind ,echoes of false promises:
    YOU CAN PICK WHAT YOU LIKE
    Just one over to win
    Come here dear I'm going to treat you today
    I'll tell you what I'll do for you
    Come here, luv, no money . . .
    Just get one in . . .
    PICK WHAT YOU LIKE
    ANY PRIZE YOU LIKE
    Roll'em down and add 'em up

If you come from WIGAN
You can 'ave a BIG 'UN
And at the back where there's still a headache
from Bitter and Younger's and pills yesterday
the carriages bump ahead in mysterious Ghost Train
                                        darkness

Screaming at painted horrors
Washleather ghostly fingers
polythene skeletons
hand slides carefully up warm nylon to warm dampness
                                        at top

In the brief intimacy
Then the sudden blinding reality
All out quickly
Pay again if you want to stay on
Bright lights smell of onions doughnuts frankfurters
My mind is crammed with stupid questions:
    What will you give us if we lose?
    What do you 'ave to do, Mister, to win?
    'ow much am they?
My mind is easily corrupted
Grateful to be fed on
    Candyfloss
    Hamburgers
    Brandysnaps
    Toffeeapples
    Cheeseburgers
    DO-NUTS
My mind is pathetically grateful for small worthless gifts
    Cinderella watches
    Glass Ashtrays
    Minature playing kards
    polythene dolls
    Plaster Alsatians *(would you like it standing up
                                        or lying down, dear?)*

kazoos that don't play
Magic Painting Books
Glass Milk Jugs
Sets of glasses
Plastic cars with no wheels
While my mind dreams of possessing huge cuddly red
and yellow rabbits
and glittering canteens of cutlery
My mind is thrown about whirling on the FIGURE EIGHT
COASTER, WALTZER, OCTOPUS, Jumping galloping horses
THE MAD MOUSE
Deafened by music from all sides
Johnny, remember . . .
She's a square,
Baby, I don't care . . .
And every day the newspaper headlines get worse
and I know that one day they'll get really bad
KHRUSHCHEV RAPES JACKIE KENNEDY
And then the old man will shuffle up an hour or two later
With his horrible smile and say
Late extra sir — 5 o'clock winner?
and I'll see the headlines
WAR DECLARED
And I'll give away all the prizes
take all the money out of the till
rush over to the awful dirty club kept by the
horrible old woman across the road
put all my money on the counter
and wait.

COUNTRY SONG

'Lily of the Valley (Convalaria Majalis, fam. Liliaceae).
Grows wild in N. England. Commonly cultivated. Flowers
in May. Berries red when ripe. Leaves particularly poison-
ous because three constituents depress the heart, like
Foxglove.'

What are the constituents that depress the heart?
the scent of lilies in darkgreen silences under trees
milkweed and ragwort and sunshine in hedges
small flowers picked amongst trees when it's raining

A year ago
You planted lilies in the valley of my mind
There were lilies at the bottom of my garden
And ferries at the bottom of my street

Now
I sit here in sunlight with the smell of wild garlic
Trying to taperecord the sound of windflowers and
     celandines

Wondering
What are the three constituents that depress the heart
Without you here in the country?

GREAT WAR POEMS

1 The same old soldiers walking along the same old skyline

2 Dead hand through the sandbags reaching out for the cream-and-white butterfly

3 mud/water under duckboards/mud/rats scamper in starshell darkness/mud/smell of shit and rotting bodies/mud/resting your sweaty forehead on the sandbags OVER THE TOP the first men in the lunar landscape.

4 'What did you do to the Great Whore, Daddy?'

5 Poppies slightly out-of-focus and farmcarts bringing in the peaceful dead.

6 The ghost of Wilfred Owen selling matches outside the Burlington Arcade.

7 Seafog. Red flaring lights from the shorebatteries. The roar of shells rattle of machineguns. Water running in the bilges. My feet slipping on the damp cobbles of the quayside.

8 DON'T BE VAGUE – BLAME GENERAL HAIG.

9 four white feathers clutched in a blood-stained envelope

10 a skull nestling in a bed of wild strawberries/boots
    mouldering green with fungus/saplings thrusting
    through rusting helmets/sunken barges drifting full of
    leaves down autumn rivers.

LOVE STORY

You keep our love hidden
like the nightdress you keep under your pillow
and never wear when I'm there

But
one sunfilled day
you took me to your magic room
at the end of the yellow corridor
and showed me enchanted stilllifes
Niveatins Bodymist sprays cold cream jars
glowing like jewels
your body singing pink in the sunlight
opening to me like the red pulsing heart of a flower
in Public Gardens
where peacocks open their thousand eyes for us
and birdpeople move noiselessly
through the dripping palmhouse
feeling your body under me
warm and alive as the grass under our feet

I LOVE YOU

When listening to Bruckner in the sunlit bathroom
When the hills and valleys of your morning body
are hidden from my gaze by Body Mist
When I don't have to ask who it is on the telephone
When we can't wait till the programme finishes
When I slip out quietly leaving you to sleep
untroubled dreams till morning in your darkened room
When I walk out into the dark shining streets
bright signs from petrolstations lamplight on leaves
hard unyielding lights from city flats

I LOVE YOU
Walking home yellow moon over the rooftops
cars crawling girls stopping everywhere smelling of you
Going off to sleep still smelling the rich luxury lather in
                                              your hair

Walking holding your mini-hand
Standing in the Saturdaymorning bank
hot with people worrying about money
Seeing half a bottle of gin smashed on the pavement
Even when seeing schoolgirls on buses
their blackstockinged knees in mourning for their lost
                                              virginity

I LOVE YOU
on trains
in cars
on buses
in taxis

I LOVE YOU

in that midnight hour
when all the clocks stopped
and it was midsummer
for ever

CAR CRASH BLUES or OLD ADRIAN HENRI'S INTERMINABLE TALKING SURREALISTIC BLUES

(for Jim Dine and Ch. Baudelaire)

You make me feel like
someone's driven me into a wall
baby
You make me feel like
Sunday night at the village hall
baby
You make me feel like a Desert Rat
You make me feel like a Postman's hat
You make me feel like I've been swept under the mat
baby

You make me feel like
something from beyond the grave
baby
You make me feel like
Woolworths After-Shave
baby
You make me feel like a drunken nun
You make me feel like the war's begun
You make me feel like I'm being underdone
baby

You make me feel like
a Wellington filled with blood
baby
You make me feel like
my clothes are made of wood
baby
You make me feel like a Green Shield stamp
You make me feel like an army camp

You make me feel like a bad attack of cramp
baby

You make me feel like
a limestone quarry
baby
You make me feel like
a Corporation lorry
baby
You make me feel like a hideous sore
You make me feel like a hardware store
You make me feel like something spilt on the floor
baby
You make me feel like
a used Elastoplast
baby
You make me feel like
a broken plastercast
baby
You make me feel like an empty lift
You make me feel like a worthless gift
You make me feel like a slagheap shifting
baby

You make me feel like
last week's knickers
baby
You make me feel like
2 consenting vicars
baby
You make me feel like an overgrown garden
You make me feel like a traffic warden
You make me feel like General Gordon
baby
like a hunchback's hump
like a petrol pump

like the girl
        on the ledge
                    that's afraid to jump
like a
    garbage truck
            with a heavy load on
                        baby

Short Poems

MORNING POEM
(for Deirdre)

"I've just about reached breaking point"
he snapped.

PERMISSIVE POEM

'Oh mummy dear' the daughter said
Dropping her silver spoon
'*Please* don't say dirty weekend
We call it our mini-moon.'

LOVE POEM
(for Sydney Hoddes)

'I love you' he said
With his tongue in her cheek.

ART POEM
(for Sandy)

The Mona Lisa isn't smiling!
Perhaps she got out of the wrong side of the canvas this
morning.

BUTTONS
Perhaps you don't love me at all,
but at least you sew buttons on my coat
which is more than my wife does.

CAT POEM
You're black and sleek and beautiful
What a pity your best friends won't tell you
Your breath smells of Kit-E-Kat.

APRIL MESSAGE

"Pack up. Your situation is untenable, your loss
                                                irretrievable
Y no hay remedio. CHANGE YOUR BEDDING!" – Palinurus
'Mr Henri's April Message will be a little late this year'

1

'April' he told us with something approaching confidence
'is the cruellest month'. 'That's as may be'
I thought
Remembering at least one April when I was happy
Thinking of salads blossoming on city tables
Of someone flying to Canada
leaving behind a sadfaced monkey to be looked after by
                                                his friends

April
When suicides blossom
                        on bridges
 Unquiet dead washed by the sea on beaches
Businessmen tread quietly through art galleries
lest they disturb the nymph sleeping by the sacred
                                                fountain
Or the beautiful lady with the face made of flowers
Sydney Carton changes his mind at the last minute
and takes to his heels down the nearest boulevard
muttering 'it is a far far better thing I do . . .'
They're putting your head on the cupwinners medals this
                                                year

April
        Turning night into May.

2

Country Poem

Owls were hooting when I went to bed
And when I got up blackbirds were singing
and I hadn't slept at all in between
Thinking about you.

3

Liverpool Love Poem

I love you
You love me
Ee-ay-addio
You
  love
   me.

4

Clouds
  tumbling over mountains
Blues
  turning grey over you
Owls
  hooting rooks cawing
Wind
  rushing thrushes singing
Water
  splashing over stones in an empty
Valley
  green with wild garlic.

"Gathering woodland lilies
Myriads blow together" — Tennyson 'Maud' XII, ii.

April/time to remember the death of January poets
April/rocks cropping through grass like teeth
April/and I'm blasting your name into limestone on distant
    hillsides
April/dogs brindled like cows running down country lanes
April/girls making the night air hideous with their thighs
April/in bluejeans plump like sardines
April/sermons in stones and malteserpackets in hedges
April/violets and woodanemones amongst the trees to send
                                      you in

   letters

6

        mornintide and eventide
        eventide and mornintide
        Death you is ma woman now
        You
           is
                ma
                    woman
                        now.

WILD WEST POEMS

1 Noon:
  2 tall gunmen walking slowly towards each other down
     Mathew St.

2 *'And then he grabbed her*   (for Leiber/Stoller
  And then   and the Coasters)
          He tied her up
  And then
          He lit the fuse to the dynamite
  And then
  And then
  AND THEN
        ALONG CAME JONES. . . '

3 William H. Bonney alias Billy the Kid hitches his horse
  to a parkingmeter strides through the swing doors into
  Yates Wine Lodge. Barmaids slowly back away from the
  counter. Drunks rush out into Charlotte Street. He
  drinks a glass of Aussie White and strides out, silent as he ca

4 POEM FOR BLACK BART TO LEAVE BEHIND ON A
  STAGECOACH
  I hope you ladies ain't afraid
  Of the wicked man who made this raid
  But I'm like nature quick and cruel
  Believe me, gals, I need them jewels.

5 The Daltons riding down Church Street/Bullets
  ricochet off streetsigns/windows full of cardboard
  Walkers bottles shatter/Bob Grat Emmett
  thunder across trafficlights at red/hoofbeats
  die away clattering down Lord Street.

46

HELLO ADRIAN
(for Adrian Mitchell)

Hello Adrian,

This is me, Adrian. I hope you had a nice Christmas as it finds us here. We had that nice Mr and Mrs Johnson to tea who's president of something but they didn't like those yellow people from across the road. Christmas had us a bit worried but Santaclaus in his big Red Cloak came down her chimney and now all those cards with cribs on won't be in bad taste after all. Very strange things have been happening lately. People keep falling off cliffs and into bed with me. Last night I met Paul McCartney in a suburban garden wearing a moustache drawn by Marcel Duchamp. I keep wanting to sign shelves of tins in Supermarkets. Everytime I go for coal the coalplace is full of dead Vietcong. Birds have eaten the berries off our plastic holly. I think it's going to be a hard winter.

Today is New Year's Day, should Auld Acquaintance be Forgot? I don't know but my stomach feels funny. I have sent messages to the leaders of the various parts of my body asking them to end the fighting NOW. There's no shillings left in the meter we'll have to roast a leg of pork over the gasfire. Someone's left the front door open O My God we might have had thieves murderers nutters queers anyone coming up here. Now someones taken the cat and left a shovel instead.

People keep offering me nebulous schemes for making my fortune in various of The Arts. A girl told me 'I had a dreadful time on Christmas Day, Uncle Gerald kept putting his hand up my skirt'. There were huge punch-ups in Woolworths on Christmas Eve. I have seen the entire Works of Charles Dickens on the telly this Christmas . . . Oliver Twist going to see Miss Havisham with Tiny Tim . . . Scrooge skating with Mr Pickwick . . . Pip stealing handkerchiefs to give to Little Nell . . . I can't stand it any longer if those Chuzzlewits call again we're *definitely* not at home. I'm making New Year Resolutions again but I'm not likely to meet her *this* year either. I'm going to have my poems on Cash's Woven Nametapes put inside schoolgirls' gymslips. I'm going to treat white Rhodesians as equals. I've forgotten all the others already.

I think Spring must be coming. She brought me a bunch of plastic violets yesterday. I can hear the noise of the ice floes breaking up on the bathroom floor. There's still no one waiting by the waterfall: I looked again today.

I really must close now as the Last Post is sounding, so hoping this finds you as it leaves me love to all at No. 18 from all at No. 64.

Adrian

City

'I hear your voice vibrate in all the worlds noises'

'Her dreams in broad daylight
Make suns evaporate'

Paul Éluard 'Capitale de la Douleur'

"Swarming city
city full of dreams
where the ghost in broad daylight
passes by the passers-by."

Edinburgh Sept. 1967 – Liverpool Sept. 1968

PART ONE

Got up went to the telephone bought some pies and rolls
    for lunch thinking of you tried to phone you they said
    you weren't there came home made some coffee had my
    lunch thinking of you.

Got washed put stuff under my arms to make me smell
    nice thinking of you got shaved put on aftershave to
    make me smell nice thinking of you listened to a record
    of Pannalal Ghosh playing the flute went out into the
    dry city afternoon thinking of you thinking of you.

Waking up with a headache from the night before
    thinking of you feeling suddenly sick not knowing
    where you are no way of talking to you no way of
    hearing from you Andy thinking I'd written a Haiku
    without knowing it and then discovering I hadn't.

Listening to Nadia sing "All My Trials Lord" in the spotlit
    church darkness thinking about the fresh downycheeked
    slightly blushing still schoolgirl girl who used to sing it
    four years ago still thinking of you.

Looking from the train window going small green fields
    glimmering like a pond with lapwings golden down on
    the mountainsides against a pale blue sky thinking of
    you coming back orderly rows of firtrees small rows of
    round trees fading into the horizon toy cars running up
    an inclined slope into the mist seeing wet platforms in
    Carlisle thinking of you sky and embankment covered
    with ferns and brambles grey seen through a green filter
    writing this poem thinking of you thinking of you.

Waking and reaching out in the early morning for the
    warm bigeyed girl who called everyone a machine and
    whose full breasts were a sleeping machine and whose
    big warm mouth was a kissing machine and whose hot
    suddenly wanting morning body a love machine I
    couldn't control still thinking of you.

Drinking whisky with Hamish after a quarrel in the illicit
    sundaymondaymorning hours listening to song after
    celtic song thinking of you eating a farewell meal with
    John and Lucy in the latenight café we go to every night
    thinking of you.

Listening to Adrian telling me about the lies they tell
    me about Vietnam thinking of you thinking about the
    napalmed children not flower children but innocent
    flowers of flame listening to a piper playing 'Lament
    for the Children' listening to Simpson playing pibroch
    'Dargai' wondering why I can't write a lament for the
    firechildren of Vietnam as beautiful as the haunted
    landscape music echoing from peak to peak and range to
    range of sound across glens of silence ageless lament of
    the mothers for the children of the first "pacification".

Listening to Mike read listening to Alan and Pete Morgan
    listening to my friends tell me the truth thinking of you
    listening to Ted Joans laughing spade hero hipster black
    flower from Africa feeding the audience poems songs
    chocolate and astonishment thinking of you thinking
    of you.

Thinking of you in the 2 a.m. slightly drunk darkness at
the top of the hill with Jim and Andy seeing old and
new town spread out in points of light beneath us under
the towering stonehenge Doric columns the sound of a
flute breaking into the still air Bartók and Debussy
moving out over the lamplit streets all night railway-
station and sleeping town.

Thinking of you drinking in the latenight empty hotel
lounge with Patrick newlymet friend but familiar face
from the telly making takeover bids for the songs of
Catullus and power struggles for control of Virgil's
'Georgics'.

Thinking of you trying to finish this poem back in
Liverpool where everyone's my friend except some of
my friends taking the flower painting I did for you
to be framed in gold like our love should be
thinking of you trying to finish this poem at the
seaside walking with the dog along the early September
already winter promenade where we walked a year
ago thinking of you trying to finish this poem
walking in the country a few late flowers and
blackberries in the hedges the hills ahead 'the spectre
of repopulation' waiting huge hawkheaded just behind
the skyline.

Thinking of you then one day an unexpected phone call
in the afterlunchtimedrinking helping another girl to
buy flowers afternoon hearing your familiar
halfforgotten voice sad but still warm faraway saying
you can't see me walking home with no mac and my
shoes are sneakers and let the rain in everyone over 30
has shoes and an overcoat except me feeling the still
warm September rain soaking through my clothes
thinking of you thinking of you.

52

Thinking of you watching Magic Roundabout me here
and you miles away hoping Florence and the boys will
look after you Dougal will trip over himself trying to
help Mr McHenry will bring you flowers but Zebedee
doesn't tell us 'time for bed' anymore.

Walking through dead leaves in Falkner Square going to the
Pakistani shop with Tony in the October afternoon
sunlight thinking of you being woken up in the two a.m.
Blue Angel rock n'roll darkness by Carl who I hadn't
heard singing thinking of you thinking of you drinking
in the Saturday night everyone waiting no party pub
walking with another girl holding cold hands in the
autumn park thinking of you walking home everynight
in Blackburne Place twilight thinking of you thinking
of you.

PART TWO

november.

the long fog echoes in from the river.

9.30
echoing schoolgirl hymnsinging voices into the mist outside
Blackburne House

leaves.

Ted and me eating Chinese roast duck in the November
afternoon.

foghorns

Beautiful angel who couldn't open the door

kissing warm mouth hard teeth eyes shining like the river
where the jetty puts out to sea in lines of lights

season of nice tits and hollow uselessness

cold streets.

meat oozing electric blood on hard white counters

tossing your red-gold hair your black cloak flying
your witcheyes laughing

frost at midnight.

the lone hydrangea holding out against the guns of winter

halfremembered kisses on the tip of my tongue

cold wind straining against the windowframe

thinking of you

thinking of you

A550	Hawarden Penyffordd	light like pale golden marmalade thrown against the road and sky
A5104	Llandegla Corwen	red leaves falling into our headlights
A494	Bala Dolgellau	the immobile lake extends its sleeping waters under the long glory of a winter moon
A487	Machynlleth Aberystwyth	waves glowing pale blue in the darkness dark figures of my friends running along the curving promenade.

factories at Widnes and Runcorn ravishing through the mist
orange Turner sunsparks on the grey river

red spot on the train window earth mist colours of autumn
landscape

loudspeakers in Crewe

pale lemon light through the dark fringed conifers on the
horizon

dinky cars bowling along the motorway

winter sunlight slanting across fields

sun through mist hurting my eyes

frozen ferns tall grass and umbelliferous plants
etched with white

thinking of you thinking of you

lamplight on hard frozen station platforms

Tintern Abbey looming out of the morning
(remembering dark eyes . . .)

and the Abbey Café
(D. and W. Wordsworth, proprietors)

spotlights playing over warm purple soft green trees

suddenly the long brown river
currents plaiting its sides

paleblue trees resting on the other side

fishermen

and one broken bridge
Chinese in the distance

ploughed fields Paul Nash hills coming up out of the mist

eggs for breakfast in Southampton
hardboiled to eat on the train

industrial watchtowers looming out of the morning

huge Martian head peering over buildings

falling into the train then washing
boiling water coming out of the tap marked C O L D

running over station bridges with whistles blowing

jumping out of taxis into trains just starting
bruising my knee

thinking of you

missing connections
waiting on stations everywhere

running over more bridges
carrying my life inside a leather briefcase

missing connections
the railways winning on frozen points

stopping me
catching trains
coming to see you

waiting for a taxi
the morning your last phonecall came

thinking of you
thinking of you

coming home

cat waiting black bigeyed in the hall
for Kit-E-Kat

going out again

leaving her rolled up sleeping
warm catdreams on the settee

thinking of you
thinking of you

PART THREE

here
in another Welsh landscape
rain
creeping quietly over the grass
through the window

thinking
of
you
coming up the path
to my
room
in the November sunset
red sky
between
clumps of trees and clouds
                    dark
against Moel Fammau

cheerful light
in the November bathroom

coming back
2 years later
thinking of
you laughing lying in the bath
        face downwards
    paddling in the shallows
        body pink and white
                glowing
    green and white tiles
            red towel
through the steam on my glasses

soft brown bodyhair
flowing like waterweed

now

the tiles still cutting back
in small diamonds
to the window
in the strong March daylight

furniture still the same

    creampainted chest-of-drawers
              (your pink
            nightdress in
               the
       3rd drawer down
    creampainted iron beds
        (paint
          peeling in places
    creampainted walls
    curtains and bedcover
        green folkweave
    blackpattern diagonal

some sounds of you
still there
among all the footsteps

           muddy boots
           on the floor
           from long walks
           along the footpath
           along the cliffedge
           with the daylight fading

or
on our last night there
after making love
you sleeping peacefully
me looking for a lost girl

nervous voices   torches   searching
cold rain   dripping trees
holding the other girl's hand
in the secret darkness
smelling of you

lost
girl found
foot of the cliff
in the early morning
huddled   crumpled   hair matted
freckled with blood and mud
the haunted eyes of a Bellmer doll

you
slipping
out
at dawn
for the last time
rain
sweeping in from the hills

coming back
in another year
in Springtime
thoughts
of
you
straying sheep
in the gardens

outside the window
clouds
lifting from the horizon
thinking of
you
in
another room

shadows
lengthening across the valley

           your little dancing step
           backwards
           as you open the door
           pink lacy knitted sweater
           (pink nylon seethru bra
           small soft breasts underneath)
           blue skirt
           black furry slippers
           hair tied back
           laughing invitation
           dancestep backwards
           opening the darkred door
           at the end of the yellow corridor

coming through the door
coming for dinner
steam on the windows
dark trees   lamplight outside
one red   one blue
plastic soupbowl
out ready on the table
closing the door then standing on tiptoe to kiss me
hands
feeling the curve
of your white nylon panties
under the skirt

sometimes not waiting
to eat
undressing each other
seeing
the familiar
underwear
body
always
for the first time

out
in the morning
hiding like naughty children
till the landlord goes out
watching for the grey car
in the driveway
(Breakfast
with Radio Caroline)
eggs
or cornflakes
in the red and blue bowls again)
little room
room with posters covering the walls
room like you
room that looks like you smells like you
room like me
room with too many blankets in summer
room with gasfire in winter
room that means we don't have to make love in an
                                        alleyway
green lane at night on the way to your bustation
room where we pick up our clothes afterwards
room tidy now for coffee
room happy sitting back feeling tired
room you smiling at me from the gastove
room five to twelve our happy bodies

room sleep now till morning hoping we meet no-one at the
                                                    bustop
room gone now
room preserved forever
because of you
because of me
because we wrote down one night everything in it
because it looked like you
even when you weren't there
room rented now like my dreams
to someone else

here
now
in our other room
March sunlight gone over the hills
line of lights down the drive
to the publichouse electric
where I'm going tonight with someone else
alone in the bathroom
thinking
of you
thinking
of
you

PART FOUR

for G.A. and M.D.

Walking along the Unter den Linden
thinking of you smelling the green
from the lindenleaves

East Berlin
May 1968

church steps still pockmarked with bulletholes

tiny shining watercolour worlds of Emil Nolde
Tahitian girls basking in the sunshine
menaced by the angry sea

on the mantelpiece

29 Grove Park
off Lodge Lane
Liverpool 8
15th September 1966

1 travelling-clock at ten to twelve
1 Ever-Ready U14 gas lighter
half a packet of elastic bands
Pot of Nivea
Jar of Pond's Cold Cream ('The 7-day Beauty Plan
42 gms net')

Max Factor Eye Makeup Removal Pads
1 packet Sungold 'Colaire'
Pond's 'Fresh Start' New Medicated Cleansing Gel
Body Mist Aerosol Perfume Spray
Body Mist Lemon Bouquet Spray
two not very sharp pairs of scissors
1 postcard of a flowerpiece by Bonnard
Coty 'L'Aimant' Hand Lotion
Coty 'L'Aimant' Skin Perfume
1 postcard 'In the Forest' by Douanier Rousseau
1 postcard of a Dubuffet mindscape

65

my keys to her flat
leather purse
Rentbook with 21 weeks paid
a fountain pen (black)
small Tupperware container with 7 shillings for the gasfire
tube of Anadin (7 left)

Pink flowers   green bushes   against whitewash wall
feet sliding through soft wet chalk
pale violet hydrangeas crowding in at the night lavatory
                                                        window
landscapes   *le Thil-Manneville*
wheat   flax   barley   oats   *par gueures*
cornfields bright for Ford Madox Brown   *Seine-Maritime*
fields bright with tractors   combineharvesters   *France*
          orange   red   yellow

on the gas stove

1 kettle, almost boiling, on rear right-hand gas burner
1 empty saucepan, used for thick Lincoln Pea Soup
1 fryingpan

                                              poem instead of
                                                 a photograph
                          green   grass   *for John and Ann*
              dappled with darkgreen shadow
empty winebottles   tablecloth   pale orange melonrinds
  Ann pink towelling dress   against darkgreen bushes
          holding Esther in pale violet dress
          one pink flower in the background

on the table

1 tinopener with bottle-opening device
1 empty pint bottle No. 1 Strong Ale
top of the bottle
2 empty glasses
2 empty coffee mugs (one brown one green)
1 lilac ribbon
small mirror
1 box Kleenex
The 'Devon Comfy' handmade comb
1 tail comb in green nylon

Cliffs white stained with red and ochre   *Varengeville*
white stones   *(for Mike and Jenny)*
sitting up like seabirds
lying like sealions
crowned with fringecaps of wet green hair
heads of Frankenstein monsters buried in the sand

on the armchair

1 pair white nylon panties
1 'no-bra' bra
1 pair stocking tights
1 vest dyed navyblue
1 green corduroy skirt
1 pr. gents' khaki denim trousers
1 gents' polo-necked black sweater with paintstains

Translating a poem Guillaume wrote for you:

My dear little Lou   I love you
My dear little trembling star   I love you
Body so beautifully supple   I love you
Deep cavern that squeezes like a nutcracker   I love you

67

Left nipple so pink and cheeky   I love you
Right nipple so delicately rosy   I love you
Right breast like champagne before its bottled   I love you
Left breast like the forehead of a newborn calf   I love you
Inner lips swollen with too frequent loving   I love you
Rounded cheeks moving exquisitely sticking out
                              so proudly behind you   I love you
Pubic hair blonde as a winter forest   I love you
Navel like a dark lunar crater   I love you
Armpits downy like a newborn cygnet   I love you
Delicate slope of your shoulders   I love you
Thighs whose roundness is as beautiful as
                    the columns of ancient temples   I love you
Ears veined like tiny Mexican jewels   I love you
Hair drenched in the blood of love   I love you
Knowing feet feet that tense themselves   I love you
Loins that straddle me loins so powerful   I love you
Figure that has never needed a girdle
                              slender figure   I love you
Back so marvellously shaped curving itself
                              for me   I love you
Mouth where I drink delights   I love you
Oneandonly glance starglance   I love you
Hands whose movements I adore   I love you
Nose so aristocratic   I love you
The way you walk dancing like a wave breaking I love you
O little Lou   I love you   I love you   I love you

on the drainingboard

1 plastic container full of Nescafé
1 tin Marvel instant non-fat milk
1 Pyrex Mixer
blue plastic teastrainer
2 faceloths 2 tablets 'Lux' toiletsoap
1 dishcloth
1 plastic container with green Wisdom toothbrush and

68

2 partly-used tubes of 'Euthymol' toothpaste
1 stainless steel Empire teaspoon
1 practically empty 2/- Squeezy
1 almost empty bottle Goddess Extra Rich Luxury
                                             Shampoo

Thinking of you   *Mr A. Henri*
seeing again the remembered   *c/o Logan*
flat roof   stonebuilt houses   *6 Summerside Place,*
garden wall   flowerbeds   *Leith,*
lilactree and lawn   *Edinburgh,*
sky lowering   *Scotland.*

in a large C&A Bag on the floor (for washing)

1pr. black-and-white nylon panties
1pr. pink and white Broderie Anglaise panties
1 pr. flowered panties
2 prs. red gingham panties
1pr. blue gingham panties
3 prs. black stretch nylon panties
1 pr. nylon stockings

Walking a year from when this poem   *Falkner Square*
                    was started   *Liverpool 8*
Summer into autumn railings not green grass
dried leaves trailing scraping along the pavement
eddying in the autumn wind at streetcorners
walking to the Sunday shops with her scarf wound round
                                    against the cold

on the floor

electric iron
raffia shoppingbasket
1 silver PVC shoppingbasket containing
oilpastels a rubber etc.
1 brush in a plastic cup of turpentine
2 pr. ladies' black shoes
2 pr. ladies' blue shoes
1 pr. white leather boots
1 pr. gents' black chelsea boots
1 pr. canvas sneakers
1 pr. black nylon fur slippers
1 wrist watch at five to twelve
1 pale blue nylon nightdress

Living now with another girl warm welcoming at five to
                                                    midnight
lopsided teddybear in a knitted overall round thighs
                                                    darkblue panties
head uplifted in pubs laughing

on the bed

1 almost new Dutch blanket
2 pillows
tangled sheets and blankets
2 people 1 male 1 female

70

THINK

Sydney Jeremy Nadia churchsongs castle slung theatrical
against the sky

THINK

Garden Flat
47 Downshire Hill
London, N.W.3

sitting finishing this poem
sunlight on Hampstead morning garden
green grass   light through leaves
white posts   one red rose
trying to forget you taking away part of me
then giving it away   shadows
chasing sunlight across the breakfast garden
Bodymist starglance leaves taxis stations
frost greenandwhite lino warmth soupbowls
one pink flower a flute Night city they said
you weren't there   1 black nylon bra (on the
armchair) fading over the hills cliffs daylight
frost   voices   darkness smelling of you

THINKING

remembered bulletholes dappled with darkgreen shadows
echoing into the mist Nadia singing wet green hair
empty hotel lounge   seeing you for the last time
or was it the time before streets a bridge junkshops
bringing you a Beatles record for Christmas wanting
to tell you what's in this poem   and can't Guillaume
combineharvesters clouds Welsh landscape (pink
nightdress) standing on tiptoe cliffedge daylight
searching Chinese bridges pagoda roast duck
railings   hair flying   leaves dripping

71

THINKING OF

stonebuilt houses Nolde girls green sea empty landscapes
cliffs stained with ochre 2 coffeemugs 1 white 1 green
frost at midnight All My Trials Lord mist gantry
bridge in Lancashire town crisscross girders over wasteground
between railwaylines near-strangers holding hands
dark crumpled varnish mummy in provincial museumcase
us in the artgallery somewhere to go to for our two hours Isis
and Osiris sharing our secret five to midnight like
a winter forest floating like seaweed night hydrangeas
at the window dry city afternoon aftershave wet chalk
cornfields cornflakes the columns of ancient temples
Moel Fammau white nylon panties cold streets ferns

THINKING OF YOU

lilactree Unter den Linden the old town lights pink towelling
dress Ann seabirds Blackburne House voices in morning fog
silence on wet afternoons hair drenched her pale face
pale brown cloak in the winter park Lowry children chimney
in the distance grass dying frost factory towers waiting
room showing you the beginning of this poem (I think)
remembering the Brown Ale bottle the railway sandwiches not
what we said going out buying rolls for lunch for dinner
steam on the window publichouse electric another girl sunlight

Thinking of you

window frame cold wind small soft breasts newborn calf
leaves dying dripping frost at five to midnight earth
goodbye station steps the last time phonecall seaside
winter promenade sunlight on leaves train rattling through
the night landscape leaves cold wind sunlight black
nylon fur slippers songs hills room rented now like my dreams
thinking of

72

pale orange violet blue nightdress on the floor grass leaves

thinking

dancestep backwards a wave breaking yellow corridor

think

leaves darkness sunlight smelling of you

think

drifting room

think

another girl

think

think

ing

of

th

i

nk

th

i

nk

i

ng

o

f

74

PETER PAN MAN

When I was three I went to the end of the road to watch
                                        the King go by
there was a lot of people and someone in a plumed hat.
When I was six, I wore a striped woolly pullover and lived
                                        at the seaside
somewhere, far-off, people died in the streets.
When I was eight I volunteered to join the army
tin hat, corkgun and all,
and received a nice letter from the Colonel
('. . . . wait until you're old enough,
and apply through the usual channels')
When I was thirteen I drew triumphant cartoons
showing weary Japs emerging from the ruins of Hiroshima.
When I was eighteen my horizon was bounded by Cézanne
                                        and T.S. Eliot.
After that I missed almost everything
(though vaguely aware of Bill Haley and the War in Korea)
Until suddenly, and too late, I put away childish things
painted H A N D S O F F S U E Z on walls and cried as
                                        the tanks rolled into Hungary
marched on marches and sat down on demos
saw people under horsehoofs
was thrown into horseboxes by reluctant policemen.
Stalin, the Uncle Joe we sang about in the war
crashed from his pillar and lay at one with the dust
The Yanks, who gave me chewing gum and nylons to
                                        peroxide girls
no longer F.D.R. but J.F.K., red against the green of
                                        Deeley Plaza
and photos of black men torn by police-dogs
I drew votive images of Guevara
and mourned for the childhood dead in Spain
Trotsky, Bakunin and Mao told me
I didn't grow up I grew down

worried about the things I never saw as a child
(though I was told off once for laughing at
mufflered clothcapped men searching for a lost sixpence
and can remember hearing rows about money
I wasn't supposed to hear)
Yes, I'm the Peter Pan Man, the Boy Who Never Grew Up
Girls didn't like me
until
Wendy laid me gratefully under an oak tree when I was 21
Since I was 35 a hundred Tinkerbells have opened their
                                        pale magic thighs for me
But
Captain Hook, no longer Stanley Baldwin or Winnie with
                                        his big cigar
Waits in the wings, his teeth bared in a T.V. Colgate smile
plans to take away the medicines, drink the children's
                                        milk,
imprison my brother workers.
At the gates of Halewood and St Helens
The Lost Boys argue furiously
not hearing the steady ticking of the Crocodile
black homburg and toothbrush moustache
munching black men with tears in his eyes.
And a hundred bowler-hatted briefcase Pirates
tear down the streets of the Liverpool I love
clutching their plans exultantly,
The Wendy-House is blotted out by the dust of falling
                                        Georgian buildings
While I sing love-poems through microphones at Festivals.
The faithful Nana has been given the humane killer
her meat makes other dogs bounce with health.
Yes Mr & Mrs Darling sold us all down the line
in 1921 and '23 and '37
in '44 and '45 and all those times since
It's me and Tinkerbell and a few of the Boys
on our own now
Crouched behind rainbow barricades of broken promises.